# TAYLOR: HER STYLE PRINCIPLES

## INTRODUCTION

She's pulled off fairytale ballgowns and bucolic boho, has pivoted from fifties florals to femme fatale frocks. You've watched Taylor Swift's wardrobe evolve over the years – now come and explore the style principles that have journeyed with her.

If you're looking for some sartorial Swift-spiration, I am pleased to say you have picked up the right book. As a fashion editor and proud Swiftie, I consider the following chapters my specialist subject. Reporting on Swift's every move, clothes wise, is part of my beat – but it never feels like work to me.

Throughout her career, Swift has developed a look that is uniquely – and defiantly – hers. She has worked with the same stylist, Joseph Cassell, since they met on a magazine shoot in 2011, and her loyalty extends to the brands, silhouettes, colours and accessories that suit her.

INTRODUCTION

Does she blindly follow trends? No – and that's a lesson in itself. Over the years, Swift has stuck to her guns and masterminded her own unique aesthetic. It is one that, despite her being the world's biggest pop act, still fashions her as down-to-earth and approachable.

In 2024, Swift's outfits were the most Googled, with an average of 89,591 searches every month. Imagine the pressure. When Swift chooses what to walk out the door in, the world is watching. There is no doubting her power as an influencer – what she wears sells out. Yet she still manages to have fun with her outfits. She never strays from fashion that makes her feel good.

This book is not a breakdown of Swift's eras and their album-led aesthetics. What I wanted this guide to do was pinpoint the wardrobe pillars that ran through all of them, to give you a real sense of her rules of getting dressed.

INTRODUCTION

If you're reading this, you are likely already a fan. There is so much to learn, style wise, from our favourite star. I hope you have the best time bringing each principle to life.

So... 𝔄re you ready for it?

# REACH
# FOR

> 'Red lipstick is my favorite kind of lipstick. When I wear it, I feel bold and strong.'

*ALLURE*, 2014

REACH FOR RED

It's the colour that inspired an entire album and the shade of her favourite lipstick. She uses it time and again to evoke emotions in her song lyrics; ditto when she wants to express herself through the medium of her wardrobe.

Ask a Swiftie who they associate with red and they will tell you, unquestionably, that it's their favourite musician. No wonder, when you think about it. Few artists can say they have as effectively – or cleverly – harnessed the hue. Swift often wears red on stage, the red carpet and even on the cover of *Vogue*. But she has also made it synonymous with her work. It is as essential to her lyrically as sartorially.

What do I mean by that? That red matters – not just in Swift's personal style, but her songbook. Thanks to that aforementioned hit record it has defined an era of her career. It features in her outfits as often as it does as a descriptive tool in her songwriting. To Swift, red can symbolise every sentiment in the arc of a doomed love affair, from passion and exhilaration, to anger, frustration and jealousy. She once said it is the most interesting colour to utilise when chronicling emotions, for all the different meanings it can represent.

This is why, within her fan base, red colours a corner of the so-called Swift-verse. Look on Tumblr. You'll find, when searching in relation to Swift, that it even comes with its own set of cosy, warm-tinted autumnal motifs (cute!).

To her fans and gossip columnists, red has become shorthand for her breakup with actor Jake Gyllenhaal, to which some of the most cutting ballads on *Red* owe their lyrics. Keep this in mind when considering how you might style out red in your own outfit over the next few pages. To Swift, it is not just a colour. It's a mood.

You probably know that *Red*, the record, is enormously symbolic for Swift. It is the album that critics have retrospectively pointed to as the moment her career went stratospheric – and proved her knack for versatility. It is the first she worked on with iconic names not just in country music but pop, too. It is the moment she inched away from the Nashville roots that had, up to that point, most significantly informed her career.

It gave rise to the smash hits '22', 'I Knew You Were Trouble' and the particularly blistering 'All Too Well' – not to mention the even more beloved ten-minute iteration on the 2021 re-record. When she released *Red (Taylor's Version)* it debuted on the Billboard 200 chart at Number 1 and stayed there for an entire week.

There's more. The colour red is a recurring motif in Swift's songs. 'Red lips and rosy cheeks' are referenced in 'Wildest Dreams' on *1989*. In 'Daylight' from *Lover*, she sings to her match that, 'I once believed love would be burning red'.

The second song on *Midnights*, 'Maroon' – a darker hue – has been interpreted as an exploration of why a relationship ended or feelings of abandonment. Swift speaks of 'rust' growing on telephones and the lips she 'used to call home'.

Yes, red is a well-worn tool for Swift when crafting her art. But as the next pages will evidence – and what we are really here to discuss – is that she wields it to her advantage just as effectively in her wardrobe.

That's why we are starting our deep-dive into her songbook of style here. Whether you think you might be more burgundy than scarlet, already dress head to toe in tomato tones or are someone who might prefer just a pop of cherry in your look, consider the next few pages your ultimate how-to with rouge (Taylor's version).

REACH FOR RED

# Taylor's TAKE ON RED

The musician's sartorial relationship with red runs deep. Swift has been wearing it since the earliest days of her career – even in some of her very first public appearances.

Take the outfit she chose to sing the national anthem in at a Philadelphia 76ers basketball game in her then-home state of Pennsylvania in 2002. The 12-year-old stepped onto the court in a long, bright scarlet cardigan with her t-shirt and jeans – a look you might argue simply paid tribute to her native country's national colours, but I suspect was put together so that, in the 22,000-capacity arena, she could be seen.

Perhaps she wanted to borrow a bit of the hue's boldness, too. It would be far from the last time she chose to wear it for public-facing events. Swift clearly recognises the power of red as a confidence transmitter: it is the perfect choice in moments one might require a little mood or mettle boost.

It has been the making of many of her red-carpet looks, be they ethereal Elie Saab ballgowns or long-sleeve Stella McCartney sequin tops. Equally spotlit has been its appearances on stage in the form of beaded Jenny Packham cocktail dresses, colour block shorts and striped tops. On the Red tour, it even appeared as a ringmaster's jacket, complete with top hat.

One of her most well-executed red-carpet looks is the one she wore to the Grammys in 2016. Swift was outfitted in a bright red-orange – let's call it coral – bralette with a dramatic hot pink, thigh-split maxi skirt designed for her by the Italian legend Donatella Versace.

Another, in 2019, was the Oscar de la Renta strapless coupé satin gown she modelled at the premiere of the musical movie *Cats*. It came in a striking floral-appliqued mix of classic ruby and burgundy. The film itself may not have received rave reviews, but Swift's ensemble went down well with critics.

What accessorised both of these outfits – and would be remiss not to mention here – were Swift's trademark crimson-painted lips. Turn to the next page for a guide on how to master those in the shade for you.

REACH FOR RED

# FINDING YOUR

So, what about the ways you might wear red? As a colour, I personally adore it. I think there is a hue and a hack to styling it for everyone, whether you're a minimalist, maximalist – or someone who sits in between.

Perhaps an easy place to start is to consider just how many shades of red there are (a whole spectrum!) and which might suit you best. Of course, this is down to which you are drawn to. Deciding what to wear is very much about how you feel in a garment. But you may also be interested in which will most nicely complement your complexion.

Everyone has different skin undertones: cool, warm, olive or neutral. Don't worry if you don't know what yours are – there is an easy way of finding out. Say hello to the paper test.

# RED

## THE PAPER TEST

In a naturally lit area, take a piece of white paper in front of a mirror and place it next to your face. If your skin looks pinkish, you have COOL undertones. If it looks yellow, you have WARM undertones. If it's green you see, you have OLIVE undertones. Those who see nothing are NEUTRAL.

If this doesn't work for you – or you want to save a tree – have a quick look at the veins on your wrist. If they appear blue or purple, you probably have COOL undertones, whereas green or yellow indicates WARM. Those with cool undertones may also find that their skin burns easily in the sun and suits silver jewellery – vice versa for those with warm undertones.

Got it? Onto stage two. I have suggested three reds that suit each undertone. Don't take it as a hard-and-fast rule, but rather some inspiration – a jumping off point if you have never experimented with red before.

### COOL undertones
**Choose blue- or purple-based reds**
Maroon—Ruby—Crimson

### WARM undertones
**Choose warm orange-based reds**
Chilli— Scarlet—Poppy

### OLIVE undertones
**Choose autumnal reds**
Brick red—Poppy—Vermilion

### NEUTRAL
**Choose any reds**
Go wild!

# FULL LOOK, OR JUST A …

There is no wrong way to wear red. If you love it, I implore you to wear it top to toe, year round, day and night. Red is rather special because, much like Taylor, it possesses the power of reinvention. It's great for cocktail hour and full of drama, but can also be a comfort blanket – the shade of your favourite cardi or long-sleeve striped top. It's festive and celebratory but also cosy. It's sensual, it's empowering and, most importantly, it's incredibly versatile. It might be just one colour but is a bit of a chameleon: depending on how you style it, it can be anything you like.

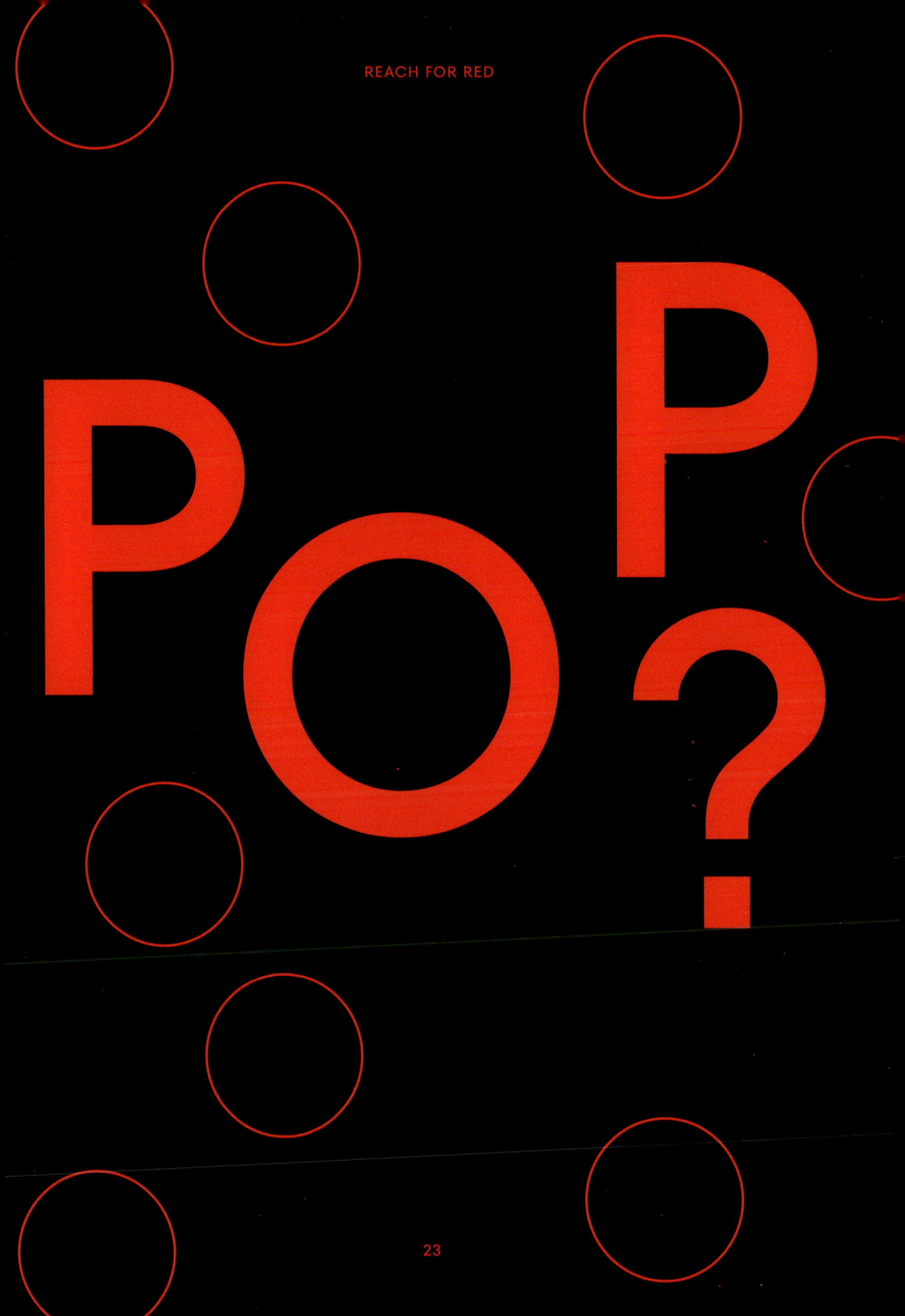

# TOP-TO-TOE RED

If you do want to colour-flood (that is, wear an entirely red outfit), I suggest mixing up your textures. This will add what fashion types call 'interest' to your ensemble, but also break it up.

SILK SHIRT
**+**
**VELVET TROUSERS**
**+**
SUEDE SHOE

CASHMERE KNIT

+

LEATHER OR SUEDE TROUSERS OR SKIRT

+

**VELVET SHOE**

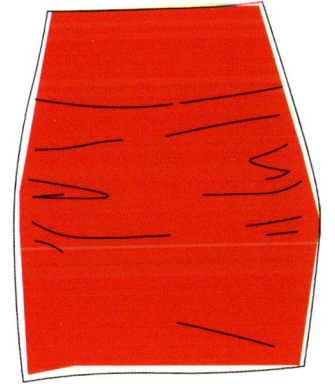

LINEN OR COTTON BLOUSE

+

**SILK TROUSERS OR SKIRT**

+

LEATHER SHOES

REACH FOR RED

# JUST A POP

For just a pop, try a red shoe – a ballet pump, Mary Jane, kitten heel, ankle boot or trainer. Nothing will dress up your favourite blue or white jeans like it. In your wardrobe, a pair of red shoes will prove a game changer. A little red cross-body bag will offer the same brightening effect. Try it if you are someone who feels safest in neutral shades.

Red is excellent on knitwear, but park any reservations you might have about naff Christmas jumpers. Chunky rollnecks, the lightest merino crew necks and soft, simple cardigans are wonderful in red tones and, again, will bring life to your blue and black jeans. You can even sling lighter styles around your shoulders in in-between-y seasons over shirts, trench coats and blazers: just knot at the neck, scarf style. This is never not a chic look.

Earrings, rings, bangles and necklaces are great places to introduce red, super subtly. Look for rubies, garnets, beads and red enamel.

# UNEXPECTED RED THEORY

Style doesn't just apply to your wardrobe – you can bring red into the home too. The 'unexpected red theory' is an interior design rule championed by Brooklyn-based interior designer Taylor Migliazzo Simon on TikTok. It suggests adding an accent, in red, to an otherwise neutral room to create energy, vibrancy – and a pop of interest that will draw the eye. It might be a border on a rug, a picture frame, a mirror frame, a lampshade or cushions on your sofa. Try it – I bet Taylor would.

# BANK ON

# BOOTS

'I'm a huge fan of boots. [...] I think they make every outfit look cooler.'

*PEOPLE*, 2011

**G**lossy ones, sparkly ones, chunky ones and pointy ones. Variations that climb so high up the legs they might as well be trousers – and several styled out not just as an accessory, but the headliner of an ensemble.

Taylor Swift's songwriting might focus on matters of the heart but there is one love affair she needn't pen lyrics about for us to know how deep it runs: that between her and a good pair of boots. Whether tall or short, lug soled or sleek, plain or crystal studded, patent or suede – there does not seem to be any hard-and-fast rules as to which models she chooses to keep in rotation. But how many pairs she does is certainly striking.

Looking through Swift's outfits over her career, it is clear not just that she feels good in boots but that they are a lynchpin in her wardrobe. She wears them with just about everything. Believe me, I have done the research: boots are a firm favourite when she is on the red carpet, and a central component in her stage costumes (see the seven bejewelled styles she had made bespoke by the luxury designer Christian Louboutin for the European leg of her Eras tour).

They are the footwear she is most often spotted out in during her downtime – almost always with shorts or a mini skirt.

Who can blame her? Boots are brilliant: comfortable, versatile, practical and useful all year round. The excellent news is that they are also incredibly easy to incorporate into your wardrobe. There is more than one way to do it like Taylor.

Ask yourself: how bold are your favourite boots? My guess would be that they might simply be black or brown. This would be no bad thing. Actually, it makes perfect sense. Boots are not just essential in most shoe-drobes, but primarily geared to shine (figuratively) in autumn and winter. Most of us want to invest in styles that stand up to those seasons, but also go with everything. It feels safer – and sounder – when boots shopping to stick to neutral colours.

Now, that approach is all well and good. I am certainly not saying these are not sensible rules to follow. But let's assume you already have that timeless, classic go-to pair in your shoe cupboard. Let's assume you might have space for another that is a little more … dazzling. Like Taylor, might you be tempted – magpie style – by metallics?

Swift knows how to make a statement on her feet. See those crystal-bedecked Louboutin pairs on her Eras stage – the black, subtly sparkling suede thigh-high style she paired with a multicoloured Versace blazer at the 2019 MTV Video Music Awards and the disco-ball mirrored iteration that partnered a matching dress on the red carpet for the 2018 American Music Awards.

# MAKE A
# STATE

# BANK ON BOOTS

These boots aren't just part of a look: they make it. Swift is drawn to boots that steal the show. It is this styling technique I'd like to suggest you can take cues from every day. Yes, even if you don't spend your working hours on stage or a red carpet.

The easiest way in is to seek out a bold ankle boot. It needn't be anything too wild – think metallic, red, white, animal print or – if you fancy it – glitter encrusted. Look for a style that you can comfortably wear with denim – whether that's a skirt, dungarees or your jeans. The idea is that they just add a bit of punch to what you already wear on a normal day, but could become your go-to for parties. It might surprise you how useful such pairs are. Don't be afraid to take a bit of a risk.

Long boots are another easy way to turn heads. They stand out more in an ensemble simply by way of the proportion of it they take up. You can stick to low-key colours in this department but for added pazazz, try glossy patent or (again) metallic or block bright colour finishes. Remember that you can always throw them on under a longer skirt or dress, revealing just a few inches: this is a technique fashion editors humorously call 'lampshading'.

# WILL YOU GO?

With so many varieties of boots available, you might be wondering where to start. There is really no right or wrong route. Swift's personal collection certainly runs the gamut of what's on offer – she chops and changes between ankle boots, calf, knee and thigh-high styles (sometimes several times in one night when she is performing).

I hesitate to use the word 'flattering' when offering fashion advice (it feels a bit dated) but there is nothing wrong with being armed with the knowledge to find clothes that make you feel like the best version of yourself. That in mind, read on for a few pointers on picking and styling out four key boot shapes – and know there is a way to wear each one for all.

## ANKLE

**Hot tip** Try to find a pair where the top of the boot ends at the smallest part of your leg, where the calf meets the ankle. A V-shaped upper will add length, if you want it.

**Look great with** Cropped trousers, jeans, mini and maxi skirts and frocks (basically, everything).

**Try** A pair in a bright or bold hue.

## CALF LENGTH

**Hot tip** Look for elasticated styles for added comfort and flexibility.

**Look great with** Skinny jeans and mini skirts.

**Try** Slouchy suede styles or cowboy boots (more on page 40).

## THIGH HIGH

**Hot tip** Pair with sheer tights and treat as trousers with an oversized blazer, shirt or rugby shirt.
**Look great with** Skinny jeans, shorts and mini skirts.
**Try** A pair in suede for added sleek.

## KNEE HIGH

**Hot tip** These are good for streamlining the leg and can make you look taller.
**Look great with** Jeans, midi skirts, mini skirts and dresses.
**Try** Preppy riding boots for extra polish.

# GO WEST

There would be no Taylor Swift without Nashville, so it would be remiss not to include cowboy boots here. One of her most iconic pairs – a duck-egg blue customised Liberty Boot Co. iteration featuring her name and her lucky number 13 – have even been displayed in London's V&A museum. She had a steady rotation of models in the early, country-centric phase of her career – usually paired with frocks, skinny jeans, sequins and an acoustic guitar.

No judgement if you have shied away from cowboy boots before. They are a relatively niche kick that are hard to separate from their original context. What they are, though, is incredibly comfortable – and easy to make look cool. You just have to outfit them in a way that they cannot be misconstrued as costume. Try a suede or gilded (yes, again) iteration under wide-leg jeans, with a mini skirt (anything but denim) or a midi with a chunky sweater, shirt or blouse. Avoid gingham, Stetson hats or pigtails – all at once, at least.

# STYLE OUT YOUR SOLE

The best thing about boots? They usually come with a heel you can't feel. Swift is a fan of platform boots from Vivienne Westwood and Stella McCartney, both of which give her extra inches without the ball-ache of a stiletto. They are easier to dance in, too.

Equally fun is the fact you can mix up the vibe of an entire outfit by introducing a boot with a particular sole. Want to toughen up a floaty midi? Just add a chunky style with a lug sole. Prefer to smarten up a t-shirt and jeans? Pop on something polished, pointed or square toed, with a little kitten heel. It's that easy. Just ask Taylor.

On which note, I have another theory as to why Swift is so boot-centric. It has much to do with another of her style principles. Could it be a coincidence that boots look particularly good paired with bare legs? So glad you asked! Turn the page and find out.

# BANK ON BOOTS

# IT'S A LEG

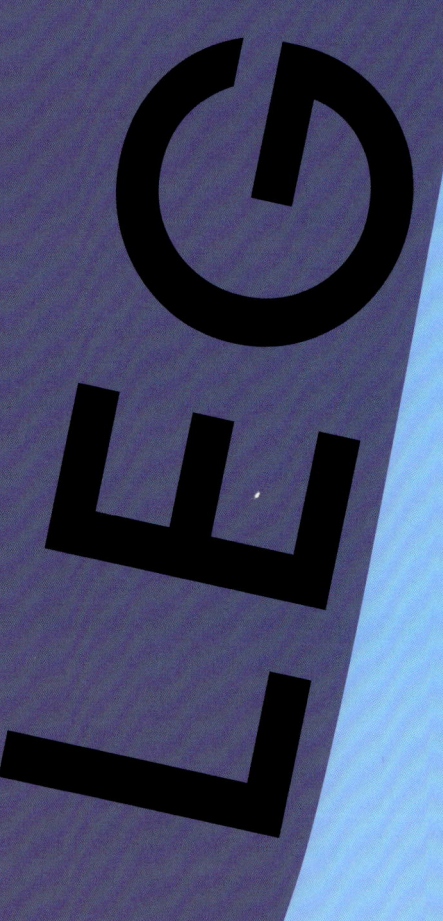

STORY

'And I think style is about more than just the clothes you wear—it's about the way you feel in the clothes, and how those clothes make you feel about yourself.'

SEVENTEEN, 2010

IT'S A LEG STORY

**T**he hemline index, a 1926 theory most commonly attributed to the economist George Taylor, states that the fashionable length of a woman's skirt directly correlates with the health of the economy in that moment – or, to put it simply, that hemlines rise and fall with stock prices.

So here's what I'd like to know: what would George Taylor, a century later, have made of the Swift-conomy? It's worth billions, it's fast growing – and driven by a certain devotee to high hems.

Have you noticed what most of Swift's outfits have in common? It was while watching her on stage during a London stop on her Eras tour that I had my lightbulb moment. The star knows when to take risks and play to her strengths when plotting her next career move and I think she is just as fearless in her approach to the bottom half of her ensembles.

Think about it: she rarely wears anything that is not designed to show off her legs.

Denim shorts, mini kilts, gowns slit to the thigh and tops re-tooled as super-short frocks. Statement tights and see-through skirts, skinny jeans, hot pants and – sometimes – no pants (ahem, that's trousers to our British readers).

Wherever Swift steps out, in whatever look, it is her pins that are the leading feature. If you ask me, she and her stylist work hard to engineer her outfits to spotlight them – sometimes in obvious ways, and at other times, ingeniously subtly.

Take when she is wearing long skirts or gowns, for example. Often the skirt will have an asymmetric high-low hem which is short at the front but long at the back, much like the white Vivienne Westwood frock she wore for 'The Tortured Poets Department' set of the Eras tour. This will have almost certainly made the voluminous, corseted garment easier to perform in. It also showed off what may be her favourite asset.

On other occasions, similarly lengthy items will be cut with a slit at the front to reveal a flash of leg. This has become a signature silhouette for Swift on the red carpet: think of her black Versace number for the 2023 MTV Music Video Awards, or the Alexandre Vauthier dress she modelled at the 2016 *Vanity Fair* Oscars afterparty. Both stand out as illustrations in how to draw the eye to the legs in maxi silhouettes.

Another case in point is Swift's outfit for the 2022 MTV Europe Music Awards. The ensemble, which was the work of the London-based Georgian designer David Koma, featured a black leotard and straight, ankle-length skirt – with a twist. The skirt itself, you see, was made not of solid material, but crystal-studded fishing-like netting. It thus showcased the bare legs it was layered over.

IT'S A LEG STORY

Even when Swift's legs are, for all intents and purposes, veiled, she has found ways to make a statement with them. The star has added plenty of skinny jeans, slim-fit trousers and leggings to her sartorial repertoire over the years, but also a collection of patterned tights. In 2024 she wore an Argyle-printed pair from Sheertex with a red Charlotte Simone shearling coat and knee-high boots to one of Travis Kelce's football games. A year earlier, while out with friends in New York, she paired a diamond-motif variation from the same hosiery brand with a Stella McCartney tweed mini skirt and matching coat.

And then there are the occasions when Swift's approach to hemlines has been more what you might call heroic. Never mind the countless times that she has opted for shorts or a mini skirt: at the 2019 American Music Awards she forwent a bottom half to her outfit at all, taking to the stage to perform in nothing but an oversized white shirt with sheer nude tights.

Similarly, in October 2023, she styled her Stella McCartney rugby top with just a pair of knee-high boots. If there was anything substantial layered beneath that thigh-skimming black jersey, you certainly could not tell.

All that is to say that Swift is engaged in a love affair with her legs. Which raises a question: how do you feel about yours? It is not a given that you'll feel comfortable showing off your knees, calves or thighs, but if that is simply out of fear or a lack of confidence, I'd like to point out that Swift has been vocal about her own battle with body image, too.

Whatever your hesitations might be, I urge you to read on. There are several possible approaches to giving legs to this style principle in your wardrobe.

# SEEK OUT SHORTS

But know that they can be any length. While Swift has a particular penchant for Daisy Duke-style denim cut-offs and hot pants – I am thinking in particular of the fifties-inspired high-waisted variety she was rarely out of during her Red tour promotion – slightly longer 'city' shorts are very elegant (particularly when you're not on a beach).

Look for tailored designs in neutral-hued structured linen or cotton twill which sit anywhere between mid-thigh and just above your knees. Satin or silk tuxedo variations are a fun alternative for evening wear. If you are keen on denim but would like a more polished alternative, simply look for pairs in white, black or dark blue washes without any rips or distressing.

In all cases, personally I would avoid anything too fitted on the leg. Those which are designed to sit a little roomier around the thigh in a subtle A-line are the most universally wearable – though it is up to you, of course.

ABOUT
# MAKE IT A MINI

Ah, the mini skirt. Swift is a fan of this garment in all its forms, be it a pleated kilt, A-line, skort (the skirt-short hybrid), denim or wrapped number, or straight pelmet. She pairs hers with crop tops and bralettes, but also fitted long-sleeve t-shirts, rollnecks, blazers, shirts and blouses. Really, she makes them work with just about anything. But what about making them perform for you?

If you want to balance out the scarcity of a mini, go for garments with a roomier fit on your top half. A broad-shouldered blazer, chunky sweater or slightly oversized, boxy shirt will do the work for you in making your mini feel a bit more grown up. Just make sure what you choose is not longer than the skirt itself (unless you fancy trying the top-as-frock look).

High-waisted styles will look longer, no matter where they sit on the leg, and vice versa. For a clean, fitted profile, look for fine-knit sweaters or tops you can tuck in (and remember, you can then throw a shrouding, oversized jacket or coat over the top – another favourite sartorial hack of Swift's).

The shoes you team your mini with will ultimately determine the vibe it translates.

TRAINERS = **CASUAL**

LOAFERS OR MARY-JANES = **PREPPY**

BALLET PUMPS OR HEELED BOOTS = **CHIC/ELEGANT**

CHUNKY BOOTS = **COOL/GRUNGE-Y**

HEELS = **DRESSY**

# TAILOR YOUR TROUSER COLLECTION

I don't mean tweaking the measurements of your favourite trews. Rather, this is about finding a pair that, in any look, will pull focus. The simplest way to do that is to hone in on fit and fabrication.

You can make a statement with the former in two ways. On the one hand, you could opt for figure-hugging skinny jeans or leggings – the kind of item that celebrates your natural shape. Or conversely, you could look at styles with an exaggerated or interesting silhouette. Flares, wide-leg, curved 'horseshoe' or barrel-leg trousers will hold court in an outfit just as effectively as anything tight. Try a selection on and find what you love most.

When we talk about fabrication, we are thinking about what the trousers are made of, both in terms of texture and aesthetic details. My advice is, if you have a particular pair you love, look for similar styles in bolder fabrics, colours and motifs. Leather, velvet, satin and metallics are my favourites, ditto animal print. A pair of subtly embellished black trousers or jeans would do the same job – just pair with plain separates to ensure they are the headline act.

# SAY PEEKABOO!

With a sheer panel, asymmetric hem or thigh split in your maxi or midi skirt, try it with tights. This is a win-win way to stick to your preferred skirt length while also nodding to this style principle.

Just a flash of leg will break up an outfit, particularly if yours has a lot of material going on. I know petite brides who have had their big white dresses tailored with a slit up the skirt – it's an effective way of ensuring they don't get lost in the frock, while also adding a bit of Va Va Voom.

Skirts with sheer or lace panels across the bottom half of the legs are another clever way to tap into this principle: they show off a little, but still protect your modesty.

IT'S A LEG STORY

# TRY IT WITH TIGHTS

The best tights are those that don't rip too easily, keep their elasticity and, ideally, are seamless. The most affordable come from Heist, Sheertex and Swedish Stockings – though on the high street, you can't beat Marks & Spencer. You might even find some studded with crystals. Such a pair would suit the next style principle.

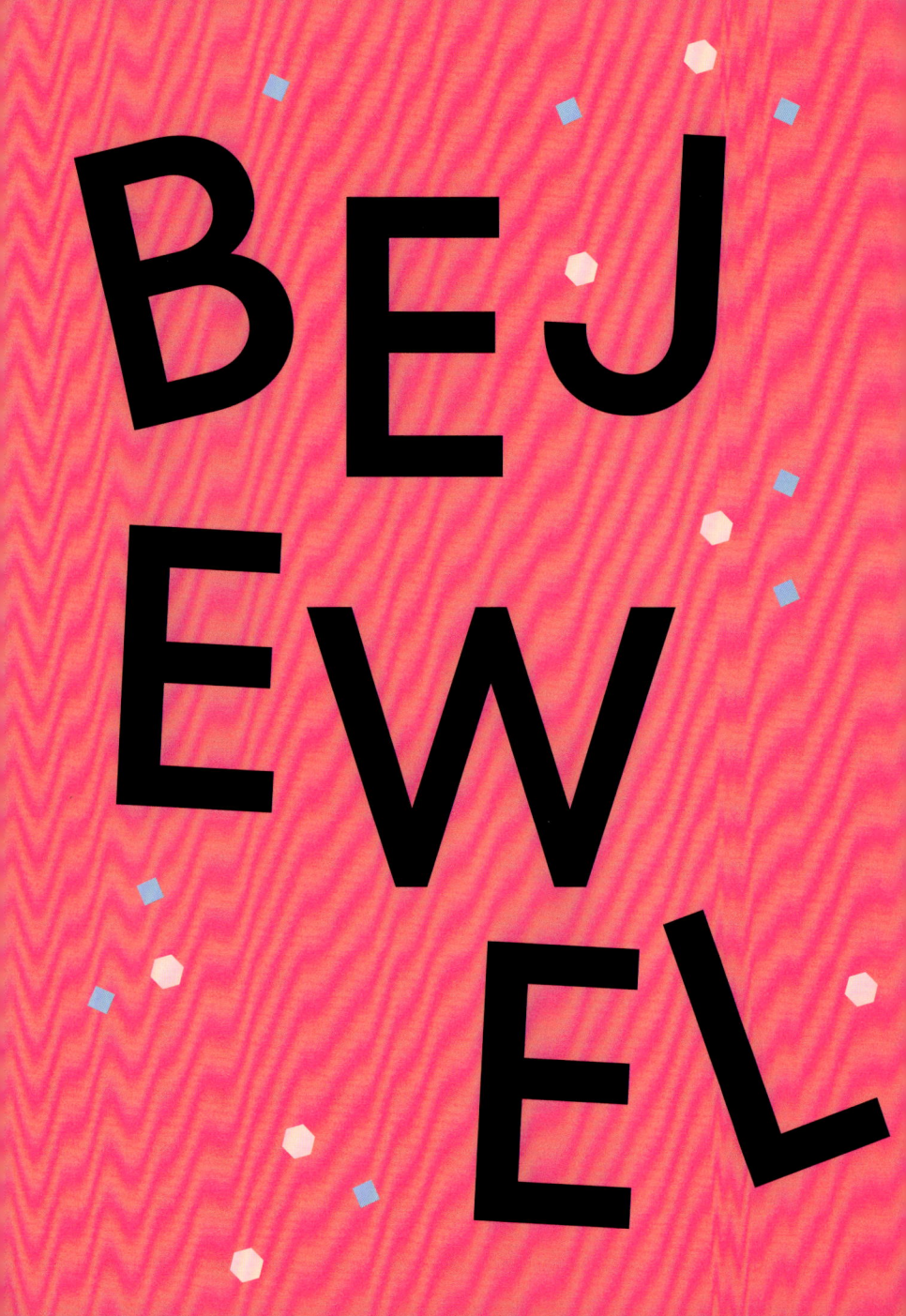

BEJEWEL YOURSELF

'I think we all know how
I feel about sequins.'

TAYLOR SWIFT, 2019

A custom Versace bodice studded with lilac, blue and pink crystals, iridescent knee-high Christian Louboutin boots and a bedazzled matching microphone. Might the most iconic image of Taylor Swift ever be that of her from the opening set of her Eras tour? For me, there is no competition. From the moment I laid eyes on it, I knew I'd never forget a look so spectacularly bejeweled.

Where were you the first time you saw it? Was it on the bus, at the office — or scrolling with a coffee in bed? Content from Eras was near impossible to escape during its twenty-one month run. Being met with an image of Swift posing in that knockout ensemble became so routine, it was almost a daily constitutional.

Snaps — professional and amateur — of the star performing in her brilliant bodysuit permeated the news cycle. They flooded social media algorithms and were readily earmarked by editors for front pages. When the tour's movie poster was released, the getup's glory was blown up to billboard proportions. Here was a 'fit so pervasive that fans even began turning up to shows in their own homemade homages. This is a level of dedication I can only respect.

For thousands of Swifties, the look is historic. It takes them back to the moment they finally saw their favourite pop star in the flesh at one of the greatest concerts ever performed (just me?). Those who were lucky enough to witness the marathon production live will recall how effective the garb was in ensuring its headline model could be seen. That's exactly what its eye-catching shine was engineered for. Even from the so-called nosebleed seats, Swift's glittering figure would have been impossible to miss.

What made it so special? There is no doubting the fact that it was high octane. But the real magic of this regalia was that, styled with loose, long hair and her trademark red lipstick, it also, somehow, managed to look effortless. Trust Swift to pull off such a glittering masterclass. She has perfect past form with shimmer – and can teach us tons about how to carry off all kinds of dazzling dress.

The star has never been one to shy away from sparkle. No, she is a self-confessed sequin addict. Her track 'Bejeweled' is an ode to rediscovering your personal power, and Swift has often played with metallics, embellishments and glitter to ensure she pulls attention – or simply give herself a glow. She has proved time and again not just how scene-stealing some well-executed spangle can be in a wardrobe – but how much fun.

We all feel just that bit more fabulous in shimmer. However, we also often make the mistake of keeping it solely for special occasions. Swift calls on killer bejewelled pieces day and night, on and off the red carpet.

For every knockout lime green sequin-saturated Gucci gown – like the one she wore to the Golden Globes in 2024 – there has been a plain t-shirt worn with crystal-studded denim shorts or embellished ripped black jeans.

On stage, all bets are off. She has serenaded stadiums with diamante-encrusted guitars, hit her marks in metallic cowboy boots and sashayed in jackets that look to be made of tinsel. The majority of her sixty-plus Eras tour costumes were splendidly embellished, from 1920s flapper-evoking gold-fringed frocks to gem-bedecked bras and mini skirts.

No other approach could have been taken for outfitting the star of such a show. But what about channelling it for your own life's headline slots? Come on: let's look at styling tricks designed to make your whole look shimmer.

# FIND YOUR METALLIC MATCH

Here's a great start to building this bejewelled principle into your own wardrobe: work out which metallic tone will work best for you. You probably already instinctively know whether you lean towards gold, silver or rose-tinted bronze tones, and personal preference is hugely important. But have you considered which might best suit your complexion?

It's worth considering. Go back to page 21 and revisit the paper test to suss out your skin tone. Gold tends to suit those with warm skin undertones, and silver those with cool undertones. Rose gold will work with both but can bring out pinkish hues in the skin, so keep that in mind.

Building gilded tones into your outfits is not limited to a pair of earrings. You should step beyond jewellery here. Metallic accessories are an editor's secret weapon: don't shy away from gold, bronze and silver handbags, belts, pumps, boots or even trainers to really lift an outfit through every season. They are magic for dressing up your old faithfuls: a t-shirt, navy jumper, blazer and pair of jeans, say.

A silver or gold blouse looks great with denim. Or how about a pair of metallic leather trousers, a biker jacket or a mini skirt? Such standout garments make a statement but you can also mix them into your look as everyday pieces.

BEJEWEL YOURSELF

# DISCO IS FOR DAYTIME, TOO

This style principle might sound best suited to parties and while, yes, shimmer-centric style is a great route to looking cool during cocktail hour, I want to get away from that limitation. You can absolutely incorporate sparkling garments into your low-key wardrobe.

The trick is simply to balance out the bejewelled elements of your outfit – or, simply put, master the art of dressing down. I've put some outfit ideas together for you.

PLAIN JUMPER OR T-SHIRT

**METALLIC TROUSERS OR SKIRT**

TRAINERS, BOOTS OR BALLET PUMPS

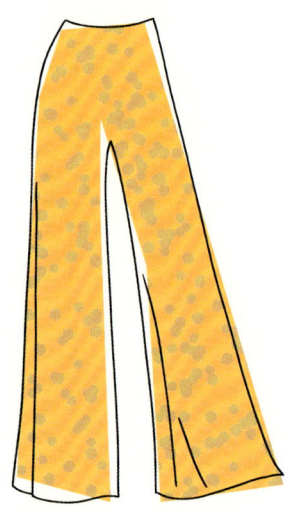

WHITE SHIRT OR T-SHIRT

**METALLIC JACKET**

JEANS

ANKLE BOOT

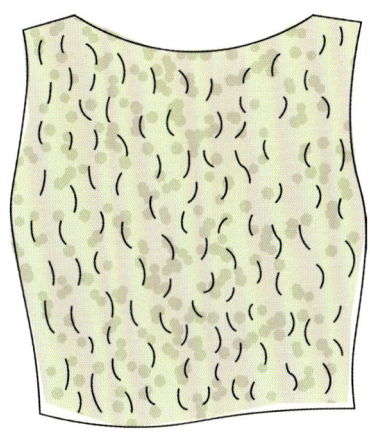

## METALLIC OR SEQUIN TOP OR KNIT
**+**

JEANS, BLACK TROUSERS OR DENIM SKIRT

**+**

TRENCH COAT

**+**

CHUNKY BOOTS, LOAFERS OR A FLAT PUMP

ANYHING YOU LIKE

**+**

## A GOLD OR SILVER SHOE

**BEJEWEL YOURSELF**

# SHOP SECOND-HAND SEQUINS

Swift loves sequins and their shimmer is certainly addictive. Unfortunately – and I hate to be a party pooper – the little plastic discs are terrible for the planet. The best way to shop for them sustainably is via pre-loved platforms like Depop, eBay and Vinted, the rails of your local charity shop – or even your best friend's wardrobe. I'm sure they won't mind if you ask nicely. It's always great to give someone else's cast-off a new lease of life. Plus, you'll be sparing the world any added plastic pollution.

Every little helps, as Swift well knows. When she wore a maroon sequin top by the eco-conscious luxury designer Stella McCartney to the 2020 Academy of Country Music Awards, it was one made of deadstock, would-be unused fabric. Here is another way to get the look without sacrificing sustainability.

You might also try to find items made with recycled sequins. Beware of 'greenwashing' from fast-fashion and high-street labels in this department – many over-promise on their eco-credentials. Shop mindfully: if a brand is producing a high volume of garments, it is probably not functioning all that sustainably. If you do want to buy new, stick to bespoke, boutique and limited-run labels. Don't shy away from spending a bit more to find something special that will last. If you ever tire of it, pass it on.

Even better, rent rather than buy. There are so many excellent websites that offer clothing loans now. They are a super alternative when you need something knockout for a big event. I rent every time I attend a posh party or wedding. It's surprising how much joy can be taken from sending a garment back – after giving it a great night out, of course.

BEJEWEL YOURSELF

# OTHER WAYS TO SPARKLE

Sequins are far from the only way of getting some sparkle. Many brands have now stopped using them entirely in an effort to be more green, instead making use of materials with shimmer sewn in. Look for garments made of lurex, lamé, metallic tinsel-y knits or drapy chainmail. When shopping, think not of one event you might wear your purchases for, but how you will incorporate them into your long-term wardrobe.

BEJEWEL YOURSELF

# LESS CAN BE MORE

Of course it can – just a touch of glimmer will loan any look a bit more glow. It could be a blouse with a bit of crystal on the collar, jeans with studs on the hems, a t-shirt with a touch of metallic embellishment or a brooch pinned to your jumper or jacket.

Whatever level of bejewelling you want to go for, be confident that any works. You'll know you've got it right when you feel that bit more fabulous – and I have no doubt you'll 'polish up real nice'.

GO

NEXT

# GIRL

# DOOR

'I like shirts and sweaters that fall off the shoulder or plaid button-ups.'

*SEVENTEEN*, 2010

We've covered the more scene-stealing looks in Swift's style repertoire, but now I want to zone in on the vanguard of considered classic pieces that make up her off-duty garb. So, what are the pillars of her workaday wardrobe?

Swift may be a global phenomenon, but when it comes to getting dressed she is just like you and me. Sure, she has a personal stylist, access to any brand in the world and a blockbuster clothing budget to spend. But study what she likes to wear when she's not in the spotlight – those rare moments she is not officially on the job (if that can ever be the case at her level of fame) – and it looks a lot like what the rest of us throw on at the weekend.

Hoodies and blue jeans; crisp white or cotton plaid shirts. Trench coats and mini skirts; denim jackets and trainers – and perfectly fitting cotton tees. Swift doesn't shy away from casual classics. What she throws on in her downtime is perfectly unassuming. It's quietly sophisticated, practical and often executed with her own brand of quirky flair. It's distinctly all-American and almost always accessible.

You might call it Girl Next Door garb.

Girl Next Door. What would you put on a Pinterest board of that aesthetic? Perhaps it's Swift in a baggy t-shirt and kooky reading glasses writing notes to her neighbour in the music video for 'You Belong With Me'. In rom-coms the classic GND is always costumed in wholesome looks that lean low key, youthful, unpretentious – and perhaps a bit twee.

Forget the stereotype. Swift's take on Girl Next Door is sweet, but also chic. Granted, it is sometimes folksy – look to the star's *Folklore* and *Evermore* cardigan-centric era. But, even so, it is refined. It is also always executed with her own twist. Swift is not afraid to embrace individuality through her style, and nor should you be.

One of the best things about our pop heroine is that she is less concerned with what is currently 'cool' than simply what she likes and feels best in. It's why her approach to dressing down is such a great lesson in building a capsule of solid style classics and putting them together in your own way.

The question is, what should be in yours? From finding your new favourite denim strides to the perfect t-shirt, let the following pages be your invisible string to a killer casual wardrobe.

# PANDEMIC PRACTICAL

The vintage-filtered, wistful and unpretentious aesthetic Swift adopted while promoting her 2020 sister albums *Folklore* and *Evermore* perfectly suited not just the records' plaintive musical mood, but also the sentiment of her fans in the midst of the coronavirus pandemic.

It was a look of minimal make-up, untamed hair, striped tops, chunky knits and jeans – a wardrobe of practical and comforting essentials which, while perhaps unexpected for a global pop star, made perfect sense in that moment. With nothing to dress up for, Swift's audience were wearing the same pieces on rotation right then, too.

GO GIRL NEXT DOOR

# DECIDE ON YOUR DENIM DIRECTION

No prizes for guessing where we'll start. There is no item more useful than a great pair of jeans. Swift knows that and my bet would be, so do you. Most of us keep at least three styles on rotation, forever going back and forth on which is our preferred pair of the moment.

That is dictated not just by how we feel in them, but the trend cycle. One minute skinny jeans are all the rage, the next, baggy barrel-leg styles are what fashion designers think we should want most. Jeans offer up a Goldilocks dilemma: shapes, fits and washes constantly go in and out of feeling just right. But how do you know when you have found 'the one'?

While what matters is honing in on fits and silhouettes that bring you the most joy, it would be remiss not to pay attention, with a light touch, to what is of-the-moment. Our jeans hold the key to making everything else we wear them with feel modern, so the trick is to find a pair that walks that line – which nods to what's modish but, most importantly, suits us.

Stylistically, jeans are a lynchpin. Shopping for them is also a minefield. But it needn't be. Over the page are a few tips that might help you narrow down your own selection or find your new go-to pair. Let's start with the waistband.

Pick your fighter: low, mid or high rise? Where the waistband of your jeans sits might be a matter of where it is most comfortable for you, but you can also take your proportions into account.

**High rise** If you have short legs and a long body, you may want to lean in a high-waisted direction – it will make your legs look longer.

**Mid rise** For long legs and a short body, a mid-rise style will balance things out.

**Low rise** This is probably the trickiest to pull off, but those with petite, curvy figures might find that it gives the illusion of symmetry between the upper and lower body. Those with straight figures and narrow hips, or simply a desire to show off their new belly button piercing, can also give it a go. Looser styles will be easier to carry.

RISE

# SILHOUETTE

I get it: with so many jean shapes out there, it's no wonder we get overwhelmed hunting for a pair that sparks joy. If you are wondering what shapes to try next, check out this cheat sheet, which outlines silhouettes worth investigating by body shape.

If you're not sure where you fit, drop into a department store and find the personal styling department. This really is worth your time. Alternatively, simply stand in front of a full-length mirror. This might sound obvious but you'll quickly get a sense of your figure.

GO GIRL NEXT DOOR

**STRAIGHT:**
Try softer shapes that hang lax on the leg: boyfriend jeans and unstructured wide-leg styles would look great.

**ROUND:**
Try straight variations if you are rounder through the middle.

**HOURGLASS:**
Bootcut jeans or cropped flares will accentuate your curves. You could also try figure-hugging skinnies.

GO GIRL NEXT DOOR

**TRIANGLE:**
If your hips are larger than your bust and shoulders, give bootcut jeans or a pair of flares a go.

**INVERTED TRIANGLE:**
If your bust and shoulders are larger than your hips, seek out a structured wide-leg design. High-rise styles are a great idea, too.

# GO GIRL NEXT DOOR

# SEEK OUT A SHIRT

Are you plain white, plaid or both? Swift is an advocate for both the classic crisp white shirt and its lumberjack-adjacent cousin. The fit of both is crucial: I always advise avoiding anything too fitted – it feels that bit more elegant. But always go with what works for you.

Lumberjack shirts are super for layering over a t-shirt. Plain cotton styles are wonderful with smart separates or jeans.

On the question of tucking in, I suggest a halfway house: the 'French tuck'. Secure just the front of your shirt into the waistband and let the rest hang loose. This offers a bit of shape but isn't restrictive.

# KNOW YOUR KNITS

Swift loves a good sweater. She understands that a simple, great-quality knit is brilliantly understated and lovely to wear: the equivalent of throwing on a warm hug. I've zoned in on her top three variations.

## Cardigan

Cardis are so versatile. They can be styled as chic, preppy, cosy – or even sexy. Try a fine-knit iteration with a little scarf tied round your neck, or wear one off the shoulder over a little lace cami. Pair with anything.

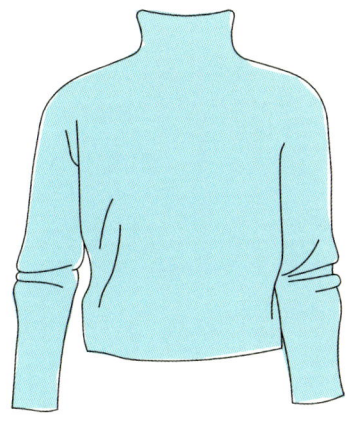

## Rollneck

Look to her 2023 Person of the Year covers for *Time* magazine for evidence of how Swift feels about rollnecks. She was pictured in two. Slim-knit styles offer a refined look, while bulkier takes are perfect for weekends.

## Borrowed from the boys

Swift loves a jumper that looks as though it has been stolen from a man's drawer (and making us guess whose). Look for an oversized V-neck cable-knit cricket jumper or big cashmere number.

## Mind the moths

Don't let your precious cashmere get munched. To keep moths at bay, remember to reshuffle your drawers every six months, keep cedar rings nearby or, for a more belt-and-braces approach, Rentokil moth-killer strips.

# GET A GREAT COAT

If you are looking for outerwear with versatility and endurability, look no further than two styles Swift favours: the trench or tailored wool overcoat. Choose one of these in a neutral style (khaki, beige, black, navy, grey) and you will have a forever outwear option that never goes out of style.

# THERE IS SUCH A THING AS THE PERFECT TEE

You want a t-shirt with the ideal fit, weight and neckline. Look for those made from 100 per cent cotton or Tencel, buy good bleach to keep your whites white and, for the fashion editor look, avoid anything too fitted or scoop-necked. Boxy is best.

# CLASSIC CASUAL SWIFT 'FITS

I think the most effective way to visualise this style principle is to see it in action. Here are some casual outfit ideas based on looks Swift has worn in the wild.

You could swap any of the elements in and out to create your own look – and you should. Consider them a jumping-off point, then play around and incorporate your own flair.

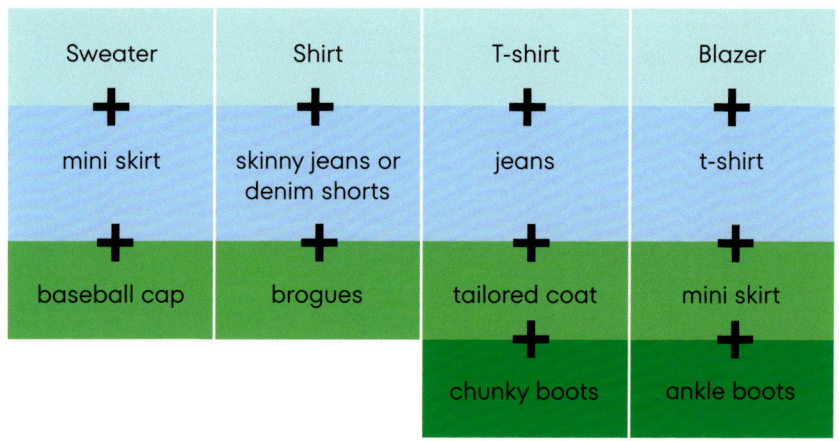

| Sweater | Shirt | T-shirt | Blazer |
|---|---|---|---|
| **+** | **+** | **+** | **+** |
| mini skirt | skinny jeans or denim shorts | jeans | t-shirt |
| **+** | **+** | **+** | **+** |
| baseball cap | brogues | tailored coat | mini skirt |
|  |  | **+** | **+** |
|  |  | chunky boots | ankle boots |

# MIX IT UP

Perhaps what makes Swift's style so approachable is the fact that she is not afraid to mix high street with high end. She is as likely to be spotted in Reformation as Dior. The learning? You don't need a luxury budget to look expensive. It might be that you invest in one thing – that pair of jeans, fabulous coat, cashmere jumper or smart shirt – and use it to elevate everything else.

# MASTERMIND YOUR

# MID

# DLE

'I've gotten more comfortable with myself, I've become more confident in my own skin.'

*VOGUE*, 2016

We're over halfway through now, which is timely. In this chapter we're going to zone in on your very own midsection. Sifting through Swift's style archive, I noticed my eye being drawn to the same central spot in so many of her outfits. It might not be obvious at first glance, but she has a signature silhouette you can trace through every era. Have you clocked how often her profile has a cinched hourglass waist?

Marilyn Monroe's was all the rage in the fifties. Over the past decade it's Swift who has quietly made the curve-creating hourglass her own. She achieves it with corsets, crop tops and cleverly placed cut-outs; empire-line gowns, protruding peplums, high-waisted separates and well-positioned belts. While the contents of her wardrobe have constantly evolved, the way she uses clothes to create shape is consistent. Her hips and shoulders tend to be cleverly accentuated by a defined midsection that is nipped in just south of her bust.

Here is yet another example of Swift finding a sartorial groove and running with it. No matter the ensemble – no matter the occasion – it almost always makes a focal point of her waist. Once you look for the details, you'll see that Swift is a dab hand at spotlighting her middle. Whether with a flash of flesh, a garment's architecture or simply an eye-catching accessory, drawing the eye to this part of her body is, I'm sure, intentional. It is a skill I think she and her stylist have workshopped over time.

If you're wondering why, consider her natural figure. There are no hard-and-fast rules for defining body types, but I do think it's useful here to observe that Swift's is what most stylists would call a 'rectangle'. Her hips, chest and waist all have similar measurements. By cinching her middle, she can create the illusion of fuller curves.

Not that she needs to, of course. But the emphasis Swift places on her middle when getting dressed is striking. Like each of the style principles presented in this book, it is a case of the star ignoring fads and focusing on fashion that gives her the most confidence. For example, no matter what denim the hip crowd is pushing, you are unlikely to catch her erring from her trusty high-rise jeans.

We keep coming back to this point, but it's an important one. The biggest lesson we can learn from Swift is to ignore the noise of trend cycles and instead lean into the clothes that simply make us feel good. Saying that, outfits that put your midriff centre stage may not be your happy place. I get it: this is the area we are most likely to feel self-conscious, or tell ourselves negative stories, about. You might have spent years shrouding rather than showing yours off. So why change now?

Because there is no reason not to. Swift herself would tell you that the only acceptable tummy is not one that is pancake flat or has washboard abs. The best way to feel good about your middle is to make friends with it. The good news is, our heroine has an entire back catalogue of ways to show us how.

So, which will you choose: fairytale corsets or cunningly subtle cuts? Turn the page. We're going to mastermind your middle.

The best way to get a sense of how you might embrace your waist is to get a better understanding of your own figure. That might sound old fashioned, but stay with me: arming yourself with knowledge of your body 'type' and how it is proportioned is the first step to getting better acquainted with it.

Think of it as meeting someone for the first time, and working out how to bring out their best. What we want to know is: where does your waist sit; how distinctive is it, naturally – and should you define it slap bang in the middle of your body, or would it be better to employ a less obvious approach?

So, stand in front of a full-length mirror. This works best either in your underwear or an outfit that allows for a clear outline of your body (say, leggings and a slim-fitting top).

Locate not just your waist (between the top of your hip bone and bottom of your ribcage), but the exact middle line of your body (usually just below the hips) and learn the difference. The latter is often the widest section of your figure. Generally we want to avoid signposting it in an outfit.

# KNOW YOUR BODY

Next, ask: are you rounder through the body (you might find it tricky to pinpoint your waist), straighter (like Swift), or does your torso in fact follow the hourglass curve? If rounder, read on to the section on empire lines, if straighter, you might find the note on peplums useful.

Finally, is your torso long or on the compact side? In laymen's terms: how much space do you have to work with? Anyone in 'camp long' can look at more exaggerated ways to cinch – belts, corsets, high-waist skirts and jeans – while those in the compact club should take a less forceful approach: think tailored jackets or even an artful tuck.

# EMBRACE THE EMPIRE LINE

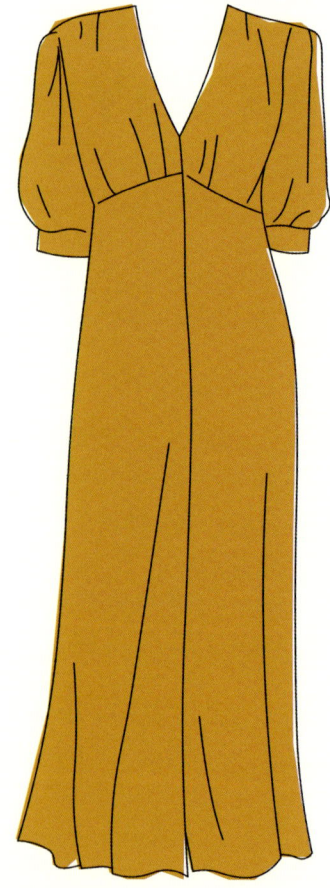

Calling all rounder figures, or simply fans of Swift's Speak Now tour wardrobe. The empire line, which nips in just below the bust and drapes delicately out below, is for you.

Look at the frocks and tops our star wore in her earliest days of fame if you need a visual. Empire silhouettes are a great option if you want to make your legs and torso appear longer, as they create the illusion of an ultra-high waist without constricting your tummy. Try also: babydoll tops and blouses.

Note – this profile will draw attention to your bust. Only you know whether that is an area you are happy accentuating.

# CONSIDER A CORSET

You could argue that Swift has always been in her corset era. The princess-in-a-tower ballgown she wears in her 'Love Story' video from 2008 is tightly girdled; so are the Vivienne Westwood variations she made a pillar of her stage and dinner-date wardrobe sixteen years down the line.

We don't tend to think of corsets as strictly daywear, but the garment does occasionally creep out of underwear drawers and into high-street collections. If you fancy trying the real deal, consider the length of your torso when shopping.

If it's lengthy, find a corset with similar dimensions. Take it from a tall gal who had this experience wedding-dress shopping: you do not want your corset to cut you off mid-stomach.

Further, don't think you need to find something firmly structured, lacy or low cut. A tailored waistcoat – longline or cropped – or soft bustier that gives a corset effect will work just as well here.

# CUT OUTS, BUT MAKE THEM COMFORTABLE

Swift loves a cut-out gown. But, as with all things, she is calculated in choosing the garments that have perfectly placed windows. Many of her red-carpet looks are proof that you can flash a little flesh and still feel comfortable.

For the American Country Music Awards in 2015, her sky blue Reem Acra dress was designed with panels that showcased just a square of her ribcage on each side. Similarly, on the Met Gala red carpet and *Vogue* magazine cover the following May, her Louis Vuitton metallic mini came with slices designed to show off just a sliver of her abdominals and back.

If you lack confidence in this area, Swift's approach is the sage one – softly does it. Find tops and dresses with what I call 'polite' panels (those that sit at the top, rather than bottom, of your torso – closer to your ribcage) which are otherwise fluid or diaphanous, for balance. This is a sweet spot for everyone and genuinely easy to pull off.

# WITH A BELT

## BALANCE IT OUT

Belts are brilliant accessories that should be used well beyond keeping your trousers in place. Used effectively, the right cincture can lend the tried-and-tested outfits you already love an easy update. Quite literally, they pull a look together.

See Swift promoting *Lover* in New York in 2019. The wide, black, gold-buckle belt she's fastened around the waist of her Stella McCartney jumpsuit for the occasion acts as a waistband, giving the outfit a bit of welcome structure – but not too much. It also nicely accents her gold ankle boots. Top marks.

Her height – 5ft 11in – and longish, straight torso are what make it really work. Belts create shape quite dramatically, so you do need to think about whether this is the right styling hack for you. Those with not quite as much space to work with around their midsection might consider looping one of a standard width around a mid- or low-rise pair of trousers or skirt instead. This will create length through the midsection. Again, it's all about balance.

# CROP, MEET HIGH WAIST

Crop tops and high-waisted separates which, worn together, only reveal a letterbox's worth of her upper torso, are a stone-cold classic combo for Swift. She's a master of revealing just the right amount of skin in just the right place and knows that high-waisted anything is a shortcut to longer legs.

If you want to try it but have your reservations, why not do so with looser-fitting items top and bottom? A boxy cropped shirt or t-shirt with wide-leg jeans, say, or midi or A-line mini skirt.

Another way in is with a cropped jacket, which will offer the same waist-signposting effect without any anxiety of getting your tummy out. Swift opted for just this sort of look when she popped to Nobu with her parents in January 2025, pairing a short, boxy black peacoat with a matching mini skirt from the NYC-based label AREA, which met at the hem with chunky chain detailing.

Sometimes a softer approach is the best one. Let the clothes do the work for you: pick out tailoring that gives you architecture all on its own (a waisted blazer, like Dior's classic Bar jacket, is the perfect option) or just tuck your top in like a fashion editor.

The 'French tuck' is beloved by stylish types. You simply fasten the hem of your top or shirt in at the very front of your waistband and let the rest of it hang loose. It breaks up an outfit without totally cutting you in half and is something of a styling unicorn: it always looks good.

# TRY TAILORING OR A TUCK

# PERHAPS A PEPLUM HEM?

Last but not least, the humble peplum. I don't know about you, but these take me right back to being a teenager, when almost everything I bought from Topshop or Lipsy came stitched with a frilled hem at the waist. Currently the style is coming back into fashion – which is just as well. Swift is a fan of it. Straighter types like her will benefit from stiffer or more exaggerated peplums, but if you already have curves to work with, consider softer, knit iterations.

GET

CO-ORD
CO-ORD

## 'I like things that are timeless, that won't go out of style.'

*INSTYLE,* 2011

Cast your mind back. It's October 2014. Taylor Swift has just released her latest – and what many critics and fans argue would go on to be her career-defining – album *1989*. It is a game changer: it debuts at Number 1 in the charts and its magnetic, eighties-inspired synth-pop sound is a statement-making departure. It is clear with this record that Swift's music, creative trajectory and positioning in the industry is undergoing a revolution – one that she is driving herself.

But look closely at what she was wearing at the time. So is her style.

It's an era of crop tops, a freshly cut sharp bob, cool winged Wayfarer shades, high heels and flouncy, thigh-skimming skater skirts. Swift is 24 years old, single, has swapped Nashville to become a newly minted resident of New York City – and is embarking on her first major fashion reinvention.

## GET CO-ORDINATED

Why? Call it what you want: simply coming of age or a carefully calculated sartorial shift. Gone are the cowboy boots, floaty tea dresses, flowing curls and wholesome, good-girl energy that have so far defined her look. In their place is a polished two-in-one ensemble that becomes a longstanding cornerstone of Swift's wardrobe.

I am talking, of course, about the high-low co-ord combo.

The Reformation teamed with H&M; Christian Louboutin paired with Prada. Swift and her stylist found a winning formula and ran with it during her *1989* era: an affordable high-street matching two-piece accessorised with high-end designer heels and handbags that carefully balanced the approachable with aspirational. It was clever. It was cool.

Most importantly, it gave her a stake in the high-fashion world while still giving her fans an ensemble they could recreate. Consider the outfit she posed in atop the Empire State Building for the launch of the record. Her tottering Monique Lhuillier heels might have cost in the region of (gulp) $700, but the white laser cut-out crop top with a matching A-line skirt from the mid-market Californian label Lovers + Friends was far more in line with her fans' shopping budgets.

A star of Swift's magnitude never does much by accident. The revamp was conceived to coincide with her pivot, musically, into pure pop – and perhaps, also, adulthood. To my mind this moment is Swift announcing to the world that she is now a grown-up. It is her asking, after well over a decade in the public eye, to be taken seriously as an adult and businesswoman

Look closely – the handbags are boxy and refined; the heels, more often than not, sky-high stilettos. The matching sets are intended to look effortlessly put together, while the choice of labels indicates a step up. She is dressing in a way that is fitting for her age, yes – but simultaneously, her far-beyond-her-years success. It is just the beginning of her commitment to the co-ord.

Like any great and enduring relationship, that of Swift's with the co-ord has proved reliable, but ever evolving. Her return to it through her own aesthetic shifts has showcased its versatility: switch up the matching set's cut, colour or print and it can mould itself into any vibe.

Take those early days. The styling of Swift's co-ords veered prim and preppy. The t-shirts, vests and bralettes paired with matching skirts and shorts were often outfitted with Alice bands and the silhouettes had a girlishness to them. Tops were cropped, skirts flounced. She favoured pastels and floral motifs. On tour, stage outfits were versions of the same but jazzed up with shimmering fringing and sequins.

Latterly, the star has opted for co-ords both soft and serious. While promoting her 2019 album *Lover*, she stepped out in Nashville in a wafty lilac cropped blouse and matching hanky-hemmed midi skirt; in 2023, she was spotted in New York in a white linen broderie anglaise bustier and midi set.

What about her adventures in tay-loring? The chevron-print blazer, flares and turtleneck she picked for her 2022 appearance on Jimmy Fallon was a slam dunk. Ditto the aubergine velvet Etro tuxedo she picked to promote the launch of her video for 'All Too Well (10 Minute Version)'. And don't forget the skirt suits. I loved the cropped check blazer and mini skirt from Vivienne Westwood she modelled at a party she threw for her Era's tour staff at the private member's club Annabel's in 2024.

## GET CO-ORDINATED

On the red carpet, Swift has shown how the co-ord can be elevated. In 2020 she paired a houndstooth-check tailored jumpsuit with a matching overcoat and court shoes. Her midnight blue sporty Roberto Cavalli long-sleeve crop top and slim-fit maxi skirt for the 2023 Grammys is another example. It fit like a second skin, its clean profile letting the sparkling embellishments shine. Super chic.

But enough – for now – about Taylor. Let's talk about how this style principle is going to work for you. It's as easy as one-two – and then just picking out a bag and a shoe. Which is not to say there aren't a few Swift-spired guidelines to keep in mind when shopping.

# PICK A SET THAT WORKS SEPARATELY

Co-ords are a beautiful thing, practically speaking: they offer the throw-on-and-go ease of a dress but can be pulled apart to work with other separates in your wardrobe.

That in mind, it's key when choosing yours to know whether the two elements of the matching set work as well as solo entities as they do in tandem.

That is to say: does the colour and print suit what you usually wear? Would it make sense to choose something cut sharply when everything else in your arsenal leans flowy? Does the cut of the skirt or trousers only work with the silhouette and length of the matching top? Are the fabric and textures aligned? Just a few useful questions to think about while browsing.

# MAKE IT MATCH

Strictly speaking, were you to ask a fashion editor, they would tell you that a co-ord and a suit are different things – but let's not worry ourselves with that level of detail. The co-ord is a close cousin of the suit: for the purposes of this style principle, consider them one and the same. The point is they are made up of two or more independent separates that match.

Co-ords come in a multitude of forms. There are so many different combinations out there, because you can create them with practically any garment pairing. Dress them up, dress them down – pack them in your holiday suitcase with a few other pieces and you've got several outfits to play with. Have a solid browse of what's in the shops.

# MAKE IT MATCH

GET CO-ORDINATED

# PLAY WITH PROPORTIONS

GET CO-ORDINATED

A co-ord can convey many things by the nature of its cut and how the silhouettes and lines of the separates work together. Swift, for example, is partial to matching a skirt or trousers with her outerwear and breaking it up with a different top sandwiched in the middle. This is a nice play on standard suiting: it looks as pulled together as any tailored set but, by replacing the blazer with a less formal jacket, shacket or overcoat, mixes up the silhouette and proportion. As a result, it looks that bit more laidback – an easy solution for everyday cool.

Shirt and trouser sets can veer from bedroom to boardroom, depending on their silhouette and what they are made of. Other key details that will alter how yours feels are the length of the skirt and whether the top is cropped – and, of course, what you accessorise with.

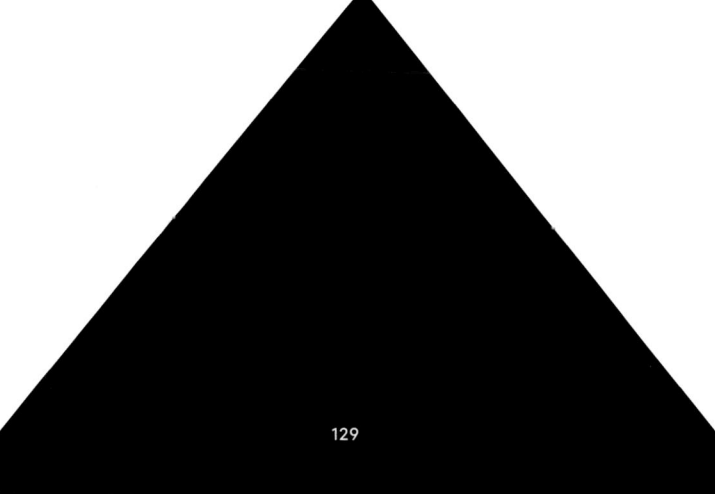

# PICK A PLAYFUL PRINT

Another joy of a co-ord is its opportunity to play with prints. Solid sets certainly offer a refined look, but there is something so jolly about a motif-stamped matching set. They are particularly great for summer occasions and sunny vacations. Try polka dots or gingham or go for animal prints or abstracts. Anything goes if it feels good on you.

# UTILISE ACCESSORIES

As ever, how you finish off your co-ord will ultimately dictate the vibe it projects on the pavement. Smarten a skirt suit up for work with heels and a boxy tote; turn it Dark Academia preppy with loafers or Mary Janes and a boxy shoulder bag. Want to ooze Parisian chic? Ballet flats and a boucle cross-body bag are all you need (a beret might be overkill, but Swift would absolutely go in for one).

If you've chosen flowing trousers and a matching shirt or a trouser suit, rely on platforms and statement earrings for parties, then swap those for trainers and gold hoops for a laidback weekend or work look. Wear the shirt tucked and untucked to alter your silhouette; push up the shirt's arms or pop the collar. These tiny tweaks make all the difference.

And what about Swift's *1989* favourite: a mini skirt and crop top? I'd try it with block-heel Mary Janes for a Mary Quant-esque sixties aesthetic or throw an oversized blazer or leather jacket over the top and consider some chunky boots to give it a modern edge.

That's not to say Swift's preference for stilettos isn't workable. It just might be easier to maintain when you are a pop star being chauffeured from A to B.

**GET CO-ORDINATED**

Yellow and black Dior tartan; stylish Stella McCartney tweed. You have to hand it to Swift: when she focuses her interests on something, she commits. One such instance is in regard to her penchant for a particular print: checks.

From houndstooth and heritage to girly gingham, there are few the star has not tried. This is good news for us: checks come in such a variety, and are so versatile, that they are one of the easiest things to incorporate into a wardrobe. Pick preppy plaid, a cheerful madras, picnic-blanket gingham, monochrome checkerboard or diamond-shaped Argyle.

Pair with plain garments, layer up different checks together or, for something different, try outfitting them with stripes. The trick is to ensure that all patterns in your ensemble have different scales – and to have fun.

Speaking of ... how do you feel about experimentation, perhaps with headwear? Time to find out.

GET CO-ORDINATED

# CHECK MATE

# HARNESS THE

# HARNESS THE HAT

'I think my style is a mix of girly, classic, and vintage-inspired pieces with a little edge to it.'

*INSTYLE*, 2011

**I**f you adopt just one accessory on your journey to Swift-ify your wardrobe, it might have to be the variety you wear on your head. From baseball caps and fedoras to beanies and bowlers, our favourite pop star is quite clear on whether or not she is a hat person.

For the avoidance of any doubt: it's a strong yes.

Is it her taste for costume drama, or just a flair for playful details? Whatever the reason, Swift has made millinery in all its forms a pillar of her signature style. Hats are very much in her fashion manifesto – and this fact is yet more proof that she is a wizard at staying true to what she loves to wear rather than choosing items because they are on trend.

But what about you – have you got many, or barely any, in your wardrobe? Hats are polarising items. We tend to naturally gravitate towards them – or not.

That's not surprising. Headwear, more than any other finishing touch to an outfit, is a form of self-expression. Most people walk out of the house with a handbag, some jewellery and a pair of sunglasses on, but – unless it's a woolly number on cold days or something required as part of a dress code – fewer of us are inclined to reach for a piece of millinery.

This is in part because of their prominence in an outfit but also because, more often than not, they are purely decorative rather than practical. In short: a lot of us feel a little 'extra' in a hat, even self-conscious. But certainly not Swift.

I think we can confidently say that our favourite pop star takes a great deal of joy from her headwear collection. Its contents range from delicate headbands and glittering circlets to baker boy and baseball caps, wide-brimmed trilbies and even cosy beanies. Lest we forget, she sent Google searches for that particular category soaring by 139 per cent in January 2025 – all because she wore one to a Kansas City Chief's football game.

She has made a great piece of headgear a regular feature of her stage costumes. Who could forget the selection of glitter-encrusted circus ringmaster top hats, designed by Marina Toybina, she rolled out on her 2013 Red tour, or the pretty floral headbands nestled into her curls while performing songs from *Folklore*?

Personally, I have an inkling that they act as a kind of armour for Swift – fashionably and figuratively. While it's true that hats can draw attention, the act of adding that extra layer must help before facing a world in which you are constantly on display. I'm no psychologist, but I'd theorise that hats aren't just in Swift's sartorial comfort zone. They may also act as a bit of a security blanket.

Perhaps you have your own standout hats that come to mind when you think of Swift. For me, it's the black trilby she wears in her music video for '22' – a version of which she gifted to one lucky member of the audience every night of the Eras tour.

The red corduroy baker boy cap she models on the album cover of *Red (Taylor's Version)* is another of my favourites, while the baggy beanies she was partial to in the noughties are reminiscent of every millennial's own indie emo phase (whether they want to be reminded of it is a different matter).

Her preferred styles have moved on some since then. These days she's more likely to be seen in a classic off-duty-celebrity baseball cap or a vintage Chanel bucket. But which should you start your collection with? There is an art to procuring the perfect hat. How you feel in it is a huge factor – it has to increase, not reduce, your confidence. But having spoken to milliners over the years, I have learned that there are other practical aspects worth considering, too.

# HEADBANDS

What about headbands? Generally speaking, I'd say they feel easier to pull off than hats. Not only are they less conspicuous, they are also more commonly worn as part of casual attire.

The main issue with headbands, in my opinion, is their connotations. Some of us put one on and feel five years old. To others they will always be synonymous with preppy Blair Waldorf sitting on the steps of the Met.

For Swift's part, she has always leaned into glitzy boho styles, worn either nestled into her nest of curls with her hair worn up, or perched directly on her forehead, hippie style. You will know whether or not this is for you.

Whatever headwear you choose to try on, a milliner will always advise you to take a view of it in a full-length mirror. This will give you the best sense of how it looks in proportion to the rest of you – and, more importantly, how you will actually feel leaving the house in it.

# FACE SHAPE

Face shape is an important aspect to consider. If you have ever struggled to find a hat or headpiece that feels like you, know that certain styles are more suited to the size and profile of your head than others. Yes, it is a bit of a science.

## Heart-shaped face

Swift, for example, has a heart-shaped face. This is revealing, because those with a heart-shaped face suit almost any type of hat. As such, if you are in the same boat, go forth and experiment. Be led by what gives you a boost – and that you can imagine slotting in with the rest of your wardrobe.

## Oval face

Good news for oval faces: they are equally versatile. You'll find most hat shapes look good, so try on a variety and, again, go with one that sparks joy.

## Long face

Like any other item of clothing, the best hats will balance and enhance your own proportions. So, if you have a long face, you might want to find a hat that adds breadth. Wide-brimmed hats are worth trying, such as panamas or fedoras.

## Round face

Panamas and fedoras are also a safe bet if you have a round face, as they add definition. Berets, pork pie models and beanies work too – all of which have been modelled by Swift.

## Square or angular face

You can look for rounded hats to soften square or angular face shapes: consider baseball caps, bucket hats or wide-brimmed panamas or trilbies.

## Petite or slim face

If you have a petite or slim face, seek out styles with a medium-size brim.

# COSTUME DRAMA

While we're here, let's talk about Swift's love of a dressing-up box. She is someone who has no problem stepping into a character – and when she decides on a moodboard for an album, she commits. It's a reminder that fashion really needn't always be so serious. So, don't be afraid to step out of your own comfort zone. Try on that colour you never normally go for; give that TikTok trend a go. You have nothing to lose by playing around with your outfits – and might even find something new you like.

# HARNESS THE HAT

# WIFT

## LOOK AT ACCESSORIES

## A SWIFT LOOK AT ACCESSORIES

'I love old-looking jewelry, whether it's an old stopwatch or key that you can put on a chain for a really authentic-looking necklace.'

*SEVENTEEN*, 2010

You've incorporated the back catalogue of her best looks into your own wardrobe playlist, now how about some bonus tracks? Accessories might be the last thing you put on, but it's often the little details in a look that are the most important. It really doesn't matter how pared-back, bijou or, conversely, eye-catchingly brilliant the styles you are drawn to might be. Throw on the right pair of earrings, shades or tote over your shoulder and you can mould your favourite jumper and pair of jeans to fit, well, just about any aesthetic mood you like.

Take it from me: even the staunchest minimalist can wield them to their advantage. Your accessories might feel like a support act, but – much like who Taylor carefully chooses to share her stage with – they should never be an afterthought. In styling, these items are powerful – not to mention fun to play around with! Consider them the tools with which to

Swift-ify your wardrobe (without even having to change anything in it).

Don't believe me? Just think of the crowds who attend her concerts. With a pair of heart-shaped, rose-tinted glasses or stack of handmade friendship bracelets, even an outfit more suited to a day at the office can be instantly transformed, ready to spend an evening singing along to 'You Belong With Me'.

This is something our star knows all too well. It won't surprise you to hear that she has some tried-and-tested final flourishes in her personal style vault. We've discussed her willingness to experiment, strong sense of self and flair for using fashion to express herself. All that plays into her approach to accessorising. She certainly, I think, has fun with it – but loyally returns to what she loves time and again.

There are practical reasons for this, of course. Like you and I, she needs to store her wallet, keys and phone somewhere. And I have no doubt that dark glasses come into their own when faced with the flashing bulbs of eager photographers.

But given how much choice Swift has – and her knowledge of how powerful her support of a brand can be – those that she is loyal to are worth noting. Like the rest of her wardrobe, I think she carefully chooses her accessories based not just on whether they bring her joy or an ensemble together, but the brand's backstory, price point and, occasionally, eco-credentials.

These are all worth taking into account when shopping for your own accessories. Here are a few liner notes for accessorising like Taylor.

# EASTER EGGS

Easter eggs are hidden signs: Swift is a savant of secret messages, known for burying clues about her life in song lyrics, videos, liner notes and even outfits that her fans like to dig out like truffles. If she wears a certain colour, print or – as at the Grammy Awards in 2024, a clock choker displaying a certain time – Swifties are quick to suss out what it might mean (ideally: a new album).

This is something everyone else can have fun with too. It could be as easy as a slogan t-shirt, getting your initials – or someone else's – embroidered on your shirtsleeve, or jewellery that literally spells something out. If you want to get something customised, look to the creator's platform Etsy, which can link you up quickly with a local maker. Even better, give it a go yourself: with easter eggs, the more personal the better.

Tell me: are you a handbag hoarder? Do you buy the same styles in ten different colourways, or are you a magpie: someone who is constantly drawn to the new, shiny and – admit it – a little impractical?

I ask because, before we dig into Swift's arm candy archive, you might want to consult your own collection. Chances are you already have one or two of the bags we'll discuss below, and this might be the perfect opportunity to breathe some new life into them. Shopping your own wardrobe is a really effective way to update your look without spending a penny. We are all a little guilty of overconsumption, so do have a dig through what you've got at home before deciding if you need to buy anything new.

Having done that, you may have found a gap that needs filling. If so, I have no doubt that the styles and designers Swift loves will provide suitable inspiration. She's actually the perfect muse in this department, for she has a real knack for picking out timeless, wearable (and what fashion editors might describe as 'anonymous') handbags. That is to say: she largely avoids ostentatious logos, sticks to understated designs, shops from brands across every budget and rewears the same models time and again.

I love this about her. It is an enormously admirable approach for a pop star with the atelier of every luxury maison on speed dial. It also makes the job of seeking out her signature It-bags that bit easier. Intrigued? Of course you are. These are the models to know.

A SWIFT LOOK AT ACCESSORIES

## TAYLOR'S FAVOURITE BRANDS

Why not start your search where we know Swift loves to shop? The designers she turns to for her most-loved leather goods are listed below. There is something for everyone: use the luxury labels for It-bag inspo, invest in an ever-after creation from one of her beloved boutique, mid-market labels or drop into Urban Outfitters, one of her preferred high-street haunts.

### £££

Louis Vuitton, Dolce & Gabbana, Stella McCartney, Dior, Vivienne Westwood, Tod's

### ££

Mansur Gavriel, Kate Spade, Aupen, Manu Atelier, Beara Beara

### £

Urban Outfitters

# TAYLOR'S TOP 5 STYLES

Now you know where to go, what are you looking for? Bag wise, these are Taylor's top 5.

## 1. The Working Lunch Tote

**Shape** Boxy, structured and undeniably ladylike, with a firm, curved top handle.
**Take inspiration from** Prada's Executive Tote.
**Size** Medium.
**How to carry** Hand held, or over the crook of the elbow.
**Great for** The office or uptown meetings: this bag means business.

## 2. The Book Bag

**Shape** Rectangular and roomy.
**Take inspiration** from Beara Beara's Noah messenger bag.
**Size** Large.
**How to carry** Cross-body or on your shoulder.
**Great for** Commuting and travelling – it's one size fits all.

## 3. The Grandma Pouch

**Shape** Retro, with a statement click clasp and thin top-handle strap.
**Take inspiration from** Vivienne Westwood's suitably monikered Granny Frame Purse.
**Size** Small or medium.
**How to carry** On the wrist, cross-body or handheld.
**Great for** Brunch with friends or a hot dinner date.

## 4. The Mini

**Shape** Any, so long as it's pocket-sized – the cuter the better.
**Take inspiration from** Louis Vuitton's Camera Box.
**Size** Small, of course!
**How to carry** By hand or cross-body, if the strap allows.
**Great for** Parties – it's designed for essentials only, more decorative than functional. Sometimes, that's exactly what you need.

## 5. The Chic Satchel

**Shape** Half-moon, bucket and slouchy.
**Take inspiration from** Isabel Marant's Oskan.
**Size** Medium.
**How to carry** Cross-body or on your shoulder.
**Great for** Everyday – there's nowhere this bag can't go. A real all-rounder (like Swift herself).

## KEEP IT SIMPLE

A note on colourways. My advice would be to seek out the more muted tones. That may not sound exciting, but Swift is someone who sticks to the classics. Beige, black, navy, maroon and dark green are safe zones that will look expensive no matter their actual price tag. Avoid too much embellishment or big logos. Simplicity is always a winner.

A SWIFT LOOK AT ACCESSORIES

# SELECT YOUR SUNGLASS TRIBE

In her *1989* era it was a classic Wayfarer. While promoting *Lover* she pivoted to the sort of shades that have become a must-have on hen-dos. Swift is also known to hide behind a pair of angular, cat-eye shades. The question is, which sunglass tribe most appeals to you?

I love Wayfarers. They really suit everyone. Ray-Ban made the square, finned sunglasses their signature in 1952, but thanks to how often she wore them to promote that 2014 album, they have become as much associated with Swift. The real ones are relatively inexpensive, last forever and have a truly timeless quality. Were you to invest in a pair, I don't think you'd regret it. To my mind, they never look anything but cool.

Another winner? Fifties-inspired cat eyes. Swift has really leaned into these in her thirties. They look great on most face shapes and in statement colourways. If your face

leans round or oval, seek out those with more pronounced points. If you're a squarer profile try on softer, rounder designs.

Thanks to the Eras tour, heart-shaped shades are also now firmly a Swift-cessory. I seem to have collated several pairs from various bachelorette parties over the years and, granted, they are not the easiest to bring out for any other occasion. They are a bit daft, but joyful – and great for holidays and festivals. I have a round face and find that the oversized iterations with a slightly more angular, triangle shape suit me best. For seventies appeal, look to those that come with slim metal frames and tinted lenses. They're great fun!

Brand wise, you are spoilt for choice. There are so many excellent affordable specialist brands out there. If you don't want to splash out on a designer pair, try Meller, Jimmy Fairly, Le Specs and Cubitts.

A SWIFT LOOK AT ACCESSORIES

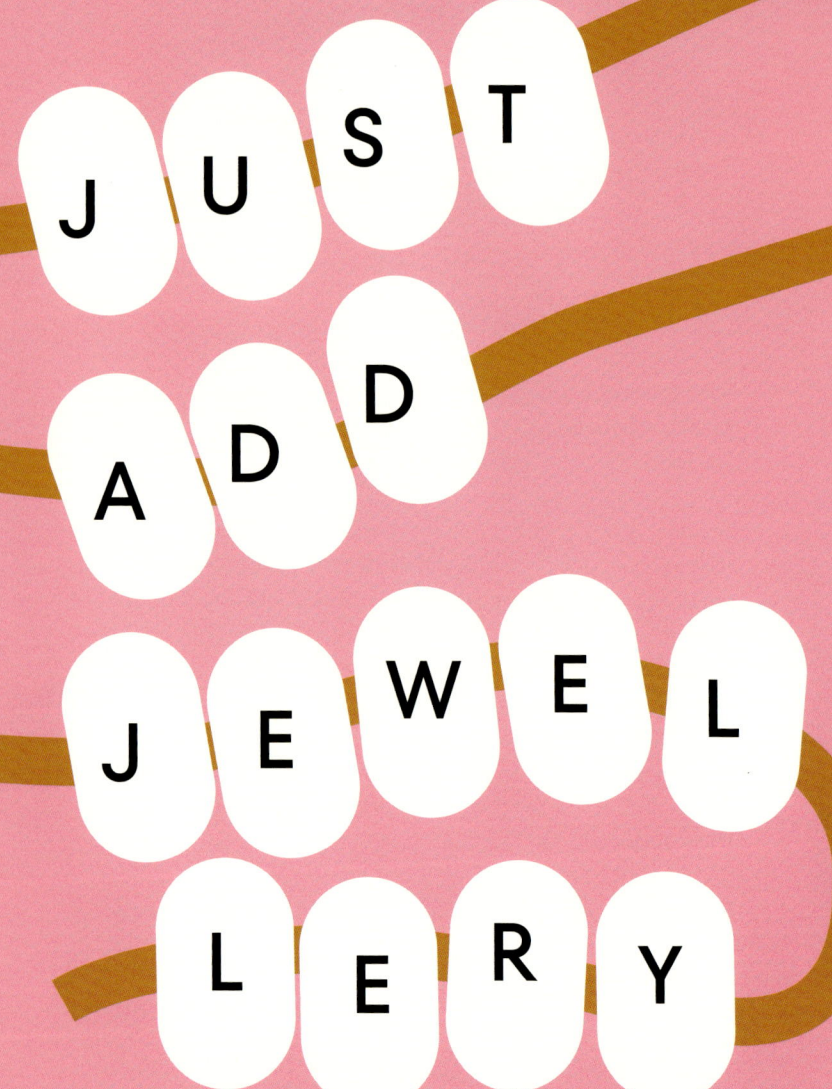

Swift takes a subtle stance on her frosting. Statement gems are not her style. She often turns to demi-fine jewellery over diamonds and would choose pieces that are meaningful over megawatt every time. We keep circling back to it, but this folds nicely into the aspirational yet approachable image she so carefully curates.

So, I'd say her first rule on jewellery is to keep it simple. Find understated pieces that you want to wear every day. It could be a delicate chain with some significant initials or a birthstone on, a simple, sculptural ring or a great pair of gold hoops with just a glint of sparkle.

As a point of experimentation, why not layer up? Swift often wears more than one necklace at a time, pairing chokers with mid-length chains and longer pendants. This is a well-trodden fashion editor styling hack and art form: on the front row, the finished result is referred to approvingly as a 'neck mess'.

If you add one thing to your trinket box, try a T-bar. Tilly Sveass, a London-based designer, makes Swift's favourite (how convenient that they have the same initials) but all-but-identical versions abound on the high street.

Finally, never forget friendship bracelets. Grown-ups can get away with them now, too. Make your own and share them with friends or buy 'adult' versions from the likes of Pandora or Roxanne Assoulin.

# BANG
## BOBS

S,

— AND THAT
RED LIP

BANGS, BOBS – AND THAT RED LIP

BANGS, BOBS – AND THAT RED LIP

# 'I love experimenting with my hair.'

*SEVENTEEN*, 2010

When we talk about someone's signature style we are never solely having a conversation about their clothes. No. If we want to get a sense of who someone is – or what they are trying to say with their wardrobe – we take in their look, top to toe, as a whole.

Think about it: if you gave two people the same blouse, they would not carry if off in an identical way. Far from it. That doesn't just come down to how it might be worn or accessorised – what colour you've painted your nails, how you've styled your hair and the mood of your make-up plays a big role in determining the vibe of your outfits too. So, in this chapter – our last – we're moving from the wardrobe to the vanity table.

Do you have a signature beauty look? Most of us don't think too much about it. We have the same trusty fixes we fall back on and go – aha! Whether you realised it or not, those everyday choices *are* your signature. No matter your outfit, it's what people come to know as *you* – whether that's a messy-chic chignon bun, perfect contouring or no make-up at all.

It's why, when we experiment with a fresh hairdo, eyeliner flick or lipstick, those who know us well really notice (and it can feel a little like we have slipped on a costume). A new fringe, shorter cut or simple switch-up of our most beloved make-up products can be a bit terrifying. We worry we'll get them wrong. Don't: it is these updates that can inject us with a real spring in our step. They are always the most modernising.

We all know what Swift's favourite grooming and glam tactics are. Hair wise, she has rarely veered from her natural shade of honey-hued blonde. She has made red lipstick her calling card, ditto an understated smoky eye and cat-eye flick. Hers is a confidently natural look. She clearly feels comfortable taking a less-is-more approach.

Not that you have to, too. It's a funny suggestion, taking inspiration from someone else's hair and make-up. How we choose to coif and powder (or not) is deeply personal, and I don't think we should start unpicking what works for us.

To be clear, this section is not a how-to in transforming yourself into a Taylor clone. But if you have long admired one of her hairstyles or are perhaps wondering how to master a bolder lipstick, this cheat sheet of tips is for you. Shall we?

BANGS, BOBS – AND THAT RED LIP

# RINGLETS, BOBS, BANGS

With her hair, Swift knows what she likes, and that's just fine. It's for that reason, though, that the world has given any tweaks to her locks plenty of attention. In most cases, these have been subtle changes in shape, length and colour. Occasionally, though, they have been dramatic.

For me, Swift's hair exists in three chapters. She's gone from mermaid waves to sharp, angular bobs and cut feathered fringes around her face – while taking her natural colour to extremes.

There is something to take from every era if you're toying with a change. I spoke with the British celebrity hair stylist Joe Pickering, who tends to the tresses of supermodels and VIPs, for his hot take.

# BANGS, BOBS – AND THAT RED LIP

# MAKE THE MOST OF

The texture of Swift's hair has changed as she's become older: what were once perm-like ringlets are now softer waves. What I love is that she always seems to embrace her hair as it is. It's never overly styled and is often just worn loose – if not shoved in a bun or pulled into a ponytail. I don't think I have ever seen it in a bombshell blow-dry, nor poker straight.

If you want to lean into letting your hair dry naturally, these are Pickering's tips.

## 1
Find good hydrating products which don't wear your hair down.

# YOUR WAVES

**2**
On wash day, remove excess water with a microfiber towel and gently brush while wet – then use leave-in products that work for you.

**3**
On days you don't have time for air drying, use a diffuser attachment on your hairdryer to help your curls maintain their shape.

Perhaps you already have curly hair. Lucky you! If you need advice for perfecting it, Pickering counsels that regular trims are key to keeping your ringlets looking fresh and bouncy. You might also want to seek out a hairdresser with curl expertise, who can recommend the right cut and products for your specific spirals.

# FANCY SOME FACE-FRAMING?

From a full fringe to cheek-sweeping curtains, Swift's bangs always bang. Have you ever experimented with them? They can be look- and mood-altering, and are often billed as a big deal. When I took the plunge and had a fringe cut in my early thirties, it changed how everything in my wardrobe looked – for the better. Even on the days I wake up and have to give my fringe a solo wash, I have never looked back. It's been way less faff than I expected.

The best thing about bangs is you can choose how bold to go with them. I personally started subtle and built up to the full shebang. The key, whether you are going in for a choppy French-girl fringe or just some soft shaping around your face, is to ensure they are cut in just the right spot. 'You are looking to complement and balance your face shape. Ask yourself what are you trying to achieve and accentuate with your fringe,' Pickering says.

**Longer faces or foreheads**
Pickering advises that a fuller style will help balance the length.

**Rounder faces** These can benefit from angled, feathered or layered takes.

## WHAT ABOUT STYLING?

'Practise, practise, practise,' Pickering states. 'It's different for every type of bang. There are some amazing tutorials online, and it's worth spending time learning what works best for you.'

Me? I rough-dry my hair and then just give the front section a zhuzh with a hot rotating hairdryer, like the Big Hair tool from Babyliss. I've also found round-edged straighteners or tongs help for a super-quick smooth-and-shape.

'If you're new to bangs, you'll find yourself touching them constantly,' adds Pickering. 'Try not to over-product them, as they will end up looking greasy.' Sound advice.

# GO IN FOR THE BIG CHOP

Who could forget the bleach and bob eras? These are the biggest changes Swift has made to her look in her career. The former was part of her vengeful *Reputation* look; the latter a fresh cut for her *1989* pop debut. But what do you need to keep in mind if you are strongly considering your own big chop?

I'll go first. Here's advice I always offer to friends heading to the hairdresser after a breakup or big life moment: 'Don't do anything drastic.'

If you are thinking of making a big change – something that will dramatically alter who you see in the mirror – ask yourself why that might be. When life is already in flux, don't overcomplicate it. A fresh trim, blow dry and gloss will perk you up, no question. A spontaneous pixie cut or dramatic dye job? I'm not saying it wouldn't look great, but if you're already feeling fragile … it could be potentially disastrous.

If you've been mulling the change for a while though and are ready for a refresh – take a seat.

'Similar to bangs, you need to think about your face shape if you are contemplating a bob,' says Pickering. 'If you have a round face, cutting your hair to sit at the jaw will accentuate your shape – whereas taking it a little longer and squarer will complement it, and vice versa.'

Thinking about going darker or brighter? Pickering is clear on this one.

'Spend the money getting it done by a professional, especially when working with bleach. Find yourself a blonde specialist who can ensure the colour suits your skin tone, is even and damage is kept to a minimum, and invest in products that will protect the colour and keep it hydrated,' he says.

If you fancy a subtle bit of blonde in your hair, ask your stylist about balayage, where highlights are painted onto the hair, rather than applied at the root. This is a great way to lift your natural colour without worrying about high-maintenance (and costly) grow-out.

# AND CHANGE

# LET GREAT SKIN GLOW

Swift doesn't wear much make-up: even on the red carpet, her glam looks low-maintenance. But she's always wearing something. She just leans on products that give her a natural glow.

This is something we can do, too. Look for water-based foundations and tinted BB creams that offer lighter coverage, then just top up where you need with concealer. Try a cream blush and bronzer over powders – these tend to be less (to use a scientific phrase) cakey. For extra sheen, a highlighter looks nice swept over cheek and eyebrow bones.

My favourite barely-there make-up brands are Ilia, Merit, Jones Road and Trinny.

# LET YOUR EYES BE THE WINDOW TO AN OLD SOUL

The word that comes to mind when I muse on Swift's eye make-up is retro. She loves a fifties flick, doe-eyed lashes, eyeshadows in warm, bronze tones and a hint of Old Hollywood gold.

This is on purpose: in 2011 she told *Teen Vogue* that she leaves eye make-up lighter to make more of her beloved red lip. This is sage advice, and speaks to that old cleavage-or-legs mantra in fashion. Everything comes back to balance.

# ROCK
## THAT RED LIP

It would be remiss not to end on the one beauty product Swift could never live without. We ran through shades of red that best suit our skin tones in Chapter One and – good news – the same logic applies to lips.

As for the application, I always think of the advice I was given by the celebrity make-up artist Julia Wren. I have watched Wren apply the perfect red lip more times than I can remember. Her top tips? Use a lip scrub prior to prep and make use of a lip liner in the same colour as the lipstick for staying power.

Now, who does Swift's lips? And what brands does she like best? It was the celebrated make-up artist Gucci Westman who first put Swift in red lipstick on the cover of *Allure* magazine: an Elizabeth Arden affair in a hue called Poppy Cream.

Since then, Swift has name-checked MAC's Ruby Woo, Nars's Dragon Girl, Pat McGrath's Elson 4, Tom Ford's Flame, Armani's Red to Go and Fenty Beauty's Uncensored. Add to cart!

## WARM UNDERTONES

= brick, cherry or rust-hued reds.

## COOL UNDERTONES

= blue- and pink-based reds, like raspberry.

## NEUTRAL

= Orange reds, mauves and berry tones.

# ENCORE!

You want more? Okay! I'll give you one more lesson in the fashion school of Swift. It's perhaps the most important, so listen closely. I think embracing all your eras is the best takeaway Taylor can teach.

Translation? Don't look back at what you once thought was cool and cringe. Lean into what you love in a given moment – and shake off what anyone else thinks. Your relationship with your wardrobe should be a love story. Fill it with pieces that make you feel great. Clothes are just clothes, after all. What makes an ensemble fabulous is who is wearing it.

Never forget that that person is you! Whatever look you are working, make sure that shines through. As Taylor well knows, your personality is your best accessory.

# ENCORE!

# REFERENCES

Chapelle, Sarah, *Taylor Swift Style: Fashion Through the Eras* (St Martin's Publishing, 2024)
Johnson, Glenys, *Icons of Style: Taylor Swift* (Welbeck, 2024)
*Rolling Stone,* '500 Greatest Albums Podcast: Taylor Swift on How *Red* Changed Everything For Her' (2020), youtube.com/watch?v=4Sn5DbZ4s2Q
*Teen Vogue,* 'Taylor Swift on Performing, Her Friends, and Favorite Songs' (2011), teenvogue.com/gallery/taylor-swift-teen-vogue-photos

# PICTURE CREDITS

Images kindly provided by: Getty (p.12 Mike Marsland; p.30 Gotham; p.43 Bauer Griffin; p.78 NCP/Star Max; p.90 Gotham; p.100 Taylor Hill; p.118 Jamie Squire; p.136 FOX; p.147 Kevin Winter; p.150 Angela Weiss; p.168 James Devaney; p.173 Rick Diamond), Alamy (p.46 Barry Brecheisen; p.62 George Walker IV; p.187 ZUMA Press) and iStock (cover background dlinca)

# DISPLAY QUOTE SOURCES

**Chapter 1**
Taylor Swift, *Allure* (2014)

**Chapter 2**
Taylor Swift, *People* (2011)

**Chapter 3**
'Taylor Swift's Style Secrets.' *Seventeen* (20 November 2010), seventeen.com/celebrity/interviews/g2057/taylor-swift-style-quotes

**Chapter 4**
Taylor Swift interviewed with Stella McCartney (25 August 2019), facebook.com/TaylorSwift/videos/431110040834972

**Chapter 5**
'Taylor Swift's Style Secrets', *Seventeen* (20 November 2010), seventeen.com/celebrity/interviews/g2057/taylor-swift-style-quotes

**Chapter 6**
Taylor Swift, *InStyle* (June 2011)

**Chapter 7**
'Taylor Swift's Style Secrets', *Seventeen* (20 November 2010), seventeen.com/celebrity/interviews/g2057/taylor-swift-style-quotes

**Chapter 8**
Taylor Swift, *InStyle* (June 2011)

**Chapter 9**
'Taylor Swift's Style Secrets', *Seventeen* (20 November 2010), seventeen.com/celebrity/interviews/g2057/taylor-swift-style-quotes/

**Chapter 10**
'Taylor Swift's Style Secrets', *Seventeen* (20 November 2010), seventeen.com/celebrity/interviews/g2057/taylor-swift-style-quotes/

## ACKNOWLEDGEMENTS

A few thank yous to the wonderful people who helped to bring this book together...

First and foremost to my wonderful agent, Florence Rees; the brilliant team at Ebury – Samantha, Emily, Emille, Ru – and my friend and fellow *Style Principles* author Natalie Hammond, who has been a part of my career from day one and put me forward to write this text.

Thank you to my biggest fellow Swiftie, Ruby, who was an excellent ear to bounce ideas (and lyric puns) off, and to my peerless colleagues and mentors at *The Times* – Nicola Jeal, Harriet Walker and Anna Murphy.

Thank you to my husband George, who makes sure the work always gets done – and helps me believe I can do it.

And finally, to Taylor Swift, of course – whose music has been the soundtrack to all the big moments in my life, including writing this book.

# ABOUT THE AUTHOR

Hannah Rogers is assistant fashion editor and stylist for *The Times* and covers whatever is contributing to the zeitgeist, specialising in trends, fashion, red carpet and celebrity. She studied anthropology and sociology at Durham University, followed by an MA in fashion journalism at Central Saint Martins, and has worked in broadsheet journalism for seven years as a writer and stylist.

POP PRESS

UK | USA | Canada | Ireland | Australia
India | New Zealand | South Africa

Pop Press is part of the Penguin Random House group of companies whose addresses can be found at global.penguinrandomhouse.com

Penguin Random House UK
One Embassy Gardens, 8 Viaduct Gardens, London SW11 7BW

penguin.co.uk
global.penguinrandomhouse.com

First published by Pop Press in 2026

1

Copyright © Pop Press 2025

The moral right of the author has been asserted.

No part of this book may be used or reproduced in any manner for the purpose of training artificial intelligence technologies or systems. In accordance with Article 4(3) of the DSM Directive 2019/790, Penguin Random House expressly reserves this work from the text and data mining exception.

Text: Hannah Rogers
Design: Claire Rochford
Illustrations: Ollie Mann
Editorial Director: Samantha Crisp
Senior Editor: Emily Brickell
Editorial Assistant: Emille Bwale

Colour origination by Altaimage Ltd
Printed and bound in China by C&C Offset Printing Co., Ltd.

The authorised representative in the EEA is Penguin Random House Ireland, Morrison Chambers, 32 Nassau Street, Dublin D02 YH68.

A CIP catalogue record for this book is available from the British Library

ISBN 9781529956429

 MIX
Paper | Supporting responsible forestry
FSC® C018179

Penguin Random House is committed to a sustainable future for our business, our readers and our planet. This book is made from Forest Stewardship Council® certified paper.